September 1968

3/6

A. P. Johnson,

c/o 17a Thurloe Place,

South Kensington

~~£2~~ £1.70

D1492677

GAUGUIN

GAUGUIN

TEXT BY

RAYMOND COGNIAT

OLDBOURNE PRESS
LONDON

PUBLISHED IN BRITAIN 1963
TRANSLATED FROM THE FRENCH
BY KENNETH MARTIN LEAKE
© OLDBOURNE BOOK CO. LTD. 1963

PRODUCED BY EDITIONS AIMERY SOMOGY,
PARIS, FRANCE, FOR:
OLDBOURNE PRESS
121 FLEET STREET
LONDON EC 4

I

Prelude
(1848–1873)

So much has been written about Gauguin in the last fifty years that it may seem superfluous to add to it. Some lives however, are so exceptional that they continue to stimulate curiosity and debate through changing periods and have to be rediscovered by each successive generation. From this point of view, Gauguin's life is one of the most significant. Research workers carefully sift through it to recover its smallest details and critics tirelessly scan his work to analyse cause and effect, because both life and work are enriched not only through the artist's own creativity, but also by potentials of which he was possibly unaware. In this way different generations can find in Gauguin the examples and lessons which they demand of the past to guide them in the future. Gauguin's life was neither constant nor unified. It reflects struggles, continual waverings, and an opposition between the man and his work that make it one of the most dramatic of all time. It is, however, these contradictions and incessant conflicts between inclination and development that finally resolved the artist's life into a complete unity entirely dedicated to the fulfilment of personality.

Continually, passionately pursuing his ideal and never wholly satisfied with his work, Gauguin was nevertheless sufficiently sure of his genius to sacrifice his entire existence to it. He was so convinced of what he had to accomplish that he fled from western civilization in the hope of discovering an illusory paradise in a more primitive world; and he renounced family ties, friendships and creature comforts. But for his genius, Gauguin would be no more than a conceited failure, embittered by his lack of success, a slave to childish egoism, burdened with hazy ideology and crude philosophy. Gauguin the artist is a triumphant image of total submission aware of its own tragic destiny, a heroic figure whose hope lies in development beyond his material life in an extension of himself; he is a visionary dedicated to his faith even when he believes he is obeying the laws of reason.

It is this double image of tyrannical egoist and lucidly inspired prophet that claims our interest–whatever the viewpoint–and the course of Gauguin's life has always provided commentators with material for new interpretations. One must try to rediscover his personal truth through this dichotomy; and the real secret lies in the bringing together of two points of view.

Gauguin's life and work are those of a man pitilessly branded by a destiny to which he is always subject–even when he believes himself to be master of it. All his decisions, whether reasoned or spontaneous, only served to confine him more vigorously within limits which seem to have been outlined from the start with absolute strictness.

Even before his birth, fate had marked him out with a mingling of the exotic and the extraordinary, with grandeur and failure often thinly disguised. Certain periods in the course of his legendary life seem to be oases of calm; they are like a haven in the shelter of which the traveller discovers the tranquillity of everyday trivialities. Such periods are peopled with characters whose simplicity leads one to expect lives devoid of adventure. In fact, these are only temporary calms and the whirling, stormy drama is soon renewed; and then even the undistinguished minor characters are forced to play parts beyond their range.

The story of Gauguin and his art is one of a man's submission and revolt. His family were distinguished by their instinct to rebel and wield authority. His grandmother, Flora Tristan, was well known for her romantic attitude to life, her social ideas, militant feminism and the passion with which she defended the cause of the workers.

She was noted for her somewhat wild liberalism and independence of spirit. Gauguin's grandfather, André François Chazal, was not particularly satisfied with his exotic wife, who was in all probability unfaithful to him. His career as a deservedly reputed lithographer was soon interrupted: he was condemned to penal servitude after an attempt to murder this colourful, seductive woman. Flora Tristan had an uncle who was Viceroy of Peru, and who died in Lima at the age of one hundred and thirteen; one of his sons became President of the Peruvian Republic. So one side of Gauguin's character may be seen to stem from his maternal inheritance.

His father's side was responsible for the calmer elements. Clovis Gauguin was born at Orléans and wrote for the newspaper, *Le National*. His career was unexceptional, apart from the fact that he indulged in somewhat free and progressive ideas, with the result that political events in 1848 cost him his job and forced him to seek a new life outside France. Counting on the support and protection of the famous viceroy uncle, he left for Peru in 1849 with his family, including Paul who had been born in Paris on June 7th, 1848.

Thus in his earliest childhood Gauguin was made aware of the hazards of a day-to-day life and the discovery of new horizons. Clovis died as they passed through the Straits of Magellan on the way to Peru. He was buried at Port Famine and, a few days later, his widow arrived in Lima with her two children, Paul and Marie. For the next six years young Gauguin lived in a sunny fairyland which he was to try to rediscover, more or less consciously, in his later wanderings about the world. We may reasonably assume that this pursuit of childhood memories played some part in his future decisions.

In 1855, Mme. Gauguin and her children returned to France with the object of settling the inheritance of Paul's grandfather at Orléans. While there she learned of the death of the great-uncle in Peru, and this meant there was no reason for leaving France again. For several years Paul stayed at the seminary at Orléans, which was a sensible counter-balance to his glowing memories of Peru. At seventeen he was engaged as a pilot's apprentice aboard the

THE SEINE AT THE PONT D'IENA (1875)
LOUVRE, PARIS

Luzitano. This was a natural result of previous events, and the voyages which he made between Havre and Rio de Janeiro were part of an initiation which, however exotic, fitted him perfectly, He joined the fleet at twenty, and when war broke out in 1870 he was a second-class sailor. After peace was signed he returned to civil life, becoming again a member of a bourgeois family. The contrasts continued. He entered the employment of M. Bertin, a broker in the rue Laffitte where he discharged his duties conscientiously, revealing himself punctual, sensible

9

and clear-headed. Earning a good salary he was able, on November 22nd, 1873, to marry a charming young Danish girl at the Mairie of the 9th district; Mlle. Mette-Sophie Gad was a Lutheran of good bourgeois family. It would seem that nothing could disturb the prospects of such a sensible marriage and such a well planned life. The young wife's calm temperament and domestic capabilities seemed to harmonize with her husband's enthusiasm for his work.

II

Birth of a Vocation
Paris (1873–1883)

Gauguin's future proclaimed itself devoid of fantasy and drama. Children were born who would probably follow the paths marked out for them as the result of their background and a good education.

Outwardly there was no shadow in the picture. Who could have foreseen any risk in the young businessman's enjoyable meetings with a painter called Pissarro? The artist was a compatriot of his mother's and belonged to the rather wild and fanciful group ironically known as the Impressionists and recently in the news. What danger could there be in Gauguin's evident pleasure in their conversation and the stimulation received that made him sometimes paint a vase of flowers, a Paris landscape, the surrounding countryside, or a portrait of his young wife?

GIRL LYING IN THE FIELDS (1844)
BUHRLE COLLECTION, ZURICH

There was no reason why he should not be interested in the arts and, moreover, his rich guardian, Gustave Arosa, collected works by Delacroix, Courbet, Daumier, Jongkind, Pissarro and Corot.

None of this affected the tranquillity of his family life. While his children grew up in comfort, the Impressionists lived in poverty. He himself was well provided for, and in one particularly successful year, he earned 40,000 francs, a considerable sum for the period. For his own pleasure, and out of kindness, he bought canvases by Renoir, Monet, Cézanne, Guillaumin, Sisley, Jongkind and Pissarro and, by so doing, did not draw much on the family fortune.

But his life began to change and in the large studio which he had arranged in his house at 8 rue Carcel, in the suburb of Vaugirard, Gauguin set to work with such assiduity that his painter friends began to look on him almost as one of themselves, though it took him a few years to gain their trust. No more than an amateur at the time of his first meetings with Pissarro, he felt his personality gradually assert itself and, in 1880, he was at last accepted by the Impressionists to take part in their fifth exhibition in the rue des Pyramides.

He offered a series of landscapes that would still appear devoid of individuality were it not that history has since disclosed the promise and originality inherent in them. In 1881 there came the first important comment from the outside world. Huysmans took note of Gauguin's canvases among those of the Impressionist exhibition, paying special attention to a nude.

He understood the exceptional feeling behind it and the realism so different from that sought after by the other artists, and spent some time over a long description of its characteristics. "None of the contemporary painters," he wrote, "who have executed nudes, have endowed them with such a strong sense of realism . . . every part of the body is shown so truthfully–the rather fat stomach resting on the thighs, the lines running down from the flaccid throat with its dark outline, the set of the angular knees and the projection of the bent wrist on the shift." This was not perhaps a very encouraging notice, but it marked Gauguin's entry into contemporary art and his desire to embrace reality as closely as possible, becoming aware of the exterior world, extracting pathos from it, and expressing his own emotions through the impact of the human figure.

So far, his artistic excursions did not presuppose any desire to rebel or escape. Nevertheless, caution and submission were less real than appearances suggested.

Gauguin's pseudo-realism was doubtless a means of escaping from the influence of his Impressionist friends, a method of taking stock of the world on his own account and discovering his own way of interpreting it. In his awareness he began to understand that the ambition which he must attain set new problems.

The years 1882–3 were decisive for Gauguin. In 1883 he left the Bourse to devote himself exclusively to his passion. "From now on," he said, "I am going to paint every day." It has often been asked what incidents led him

STILL-LIFE DEDICATED TO SCHUFFENECKER (1884)
PRIVATE COLLECTION, U.S.A.

to take such a strong decision. Was it a question of his
sense of vocation being so powerful that he had no
strength to resist it, or did other circumstances cause the
break to come easily? Charles Chassé notes that there was
a momentous financial crash in 1882 which would probably have endangered any broker's future. Faced with
the risks of what now appeared a hazardous profession,

14

FLOWERS (1885)
MR. & MRS. ROBERT WINTHROP COLLECTION, NEW YORK ▸

it is possible that Gauguin turned to one which would bring him more intellectual pleasure.

Mme. Ursula Frances Marks-Vandenbroucke has recently given valuable information regarding the anxieties that disturbed financial circles during this period and the prolonged business slump.

In her opinion Gauguin's "liberation" was imposed on him by outside events and was not a deliberate act on his part. However this may be, Gauguin clearly had courage in embarking so coolly and irrevocably on a new existence which he realised was risky. For he had been a witness to the years of poverty suffered by his Impressionist friends. He was now nearly thirty-five. His actions were not the result of youthful impulse, but the consideration of a mature man. He decided to become an artist, regardless of the advantages of his bourgeois life and the immediate interests of his wife and children.

III

The Arduous Freedom of a Painter
Rouen, Copenhagen (1883–1885)

Gauguin's decision to make a total break with his bourgeois existence is clearly one of the principal acts of his
life. He was obeying a certainty, not an impulse. Yet we
may suppose that, although he embarked on this hazardous adventure with passionate conviction, he was still
not master of his technique. His art remained similar to
that of his friends and was too greatly influenced by ex-
ternal trends for one as lucid as he not to realize his de-
pendence.

He felt the need to dedicate himself entirely to a painter's vocation without knowing as yet what form it would
take nor whether he would be able to discover a style
exactly suited to his aims and temperament. He followed
his instinct, sacrificing everything to the immediate pleasure of his own expansion, and this caused him to cast off
his everyday cares with indifference. His scorn for material
things was so overriding that he had no hesitation in in-
volving his whole family, even though they were unpre-
pared to share such trials. His wife had such trust in her
husband that she accepted the changed conditions and
pledged herself to a joint future which in no way suited
her personality. They had immediately to give up the fine
house and large studio in Paris to find a less expensive re-
fuge in the provinces. They spent eight months in Nor-
mandy, mainly at Rouen, but this time was not wholly

THE BATHERS (1885)
PRINCE MATSUKATA COLLECTION

decisive and gave no indication of the prospect of a stable life, even on a modest scale.

Mette Gauguin turned to the friends with whom she had kept in touch in her native Denmark and thought she would be able to find there a favourable welcome near her own family.

Soon Gauguin with his wife and children were installed in Copenhagen where they rediscovered the mild bourgeois atmosphere which they had previously enjoyed, but without the breath of originality that the contact with the Impressionist painters had introduced in Paris. Gauguin's bohemianism was at odds with the serious, practical nature of the Danish families around him. The material aspect of life was difficult, the sentimental side monotonous, the moral, suffocating.

The contrast became more and more marked between the Gauguin of the past and the Gauguin of the present, between the smiling young girl who had married a young, conscientious bank employee and the wife baffled by this other character who rebelled against conventions and displayed hostility towards his social milieu. The matter-of-fact beliefs, the strict morality of the Lutherans caused them to become unexpectedly opposed to a surge of uncontrollable paganism in a young man who had showed no such signs at the time of his marriage. The good sense of Mette and her friends first silenced Gauguin but then provoked him. His sense of independence became a revolt which surprised and then shocked Mette and her family.

Halfway through 1885 it seemed wise to agree to a temporary separation. Gauguin was to return to Paris where he would try to gain and consolidate the position to which he considered he had a right among the young artists. Mette would remain in Denmark where she could more easily bring up the children, at the same time considerably lightening the artist's financial burden and freeing him

FARMS AT MARTINIQUE (1887)
PRIVATE COLLECTION, BERNE

from family responsibilities. Their six-year old son, Clovis, who had been born in 1879, was to accompany his father; the other four children, Aline, Emile, Paul and Jean, were to remain in Denmark.

Gauguin's arrival in Paris was the start of his period of great poverty and his stern battle for independence. His stay in Denmark was his last attempt to avoid breaking with his family life and social background, to stop himself from withdrawing into the egoism of his vocation and to try to adapt it to the demands of society.

His return to Paris was a fresh step towards a rupture with the civilized world as we know it, but it was not a total break. For several years he had to undergo further trials before acquiring the independence of which he felt an inner need.

He wished passionately to attain it, but it could for him only come about through the deepest anguish; it was as if, in these ordeals, he had to find a stimulant to lend greater strength to the freeing of his personality.

BRETON LANDSCAPE (1888)
PRINCE MATSUKATA COLLECTION

IV

The Experience of Poverty
Paris, Brittany (1885–1886)

This period is the real beginning of Gauguin's life. His previous trials had been no more than preludes, attempts to gain freedom, and skirmishes with existence. His painting now shows signs of a renewed self-assertion. He had no positive idea of breaking away from Impressionism, however, and was probably unaware that he would react against it.

The smallest and even the least savoury details of existence are, however, preordained: by contrast with the hardships to come, those of the preceding years were no more than inconvenient periods of hopeful waiting. Gauguin was now to come to grips with real povety. It was as if, at each desperate step, fate tried to force him to renounce his stubborn attitude.

When his son Clovis fell ill, Gauguin was destitute and took a job as a billposter at five francs a day. The boy recovered and was sent to a boarding school in a Paris suburb where be slowly convalesced. Then it was his father's turn to become an invalid.

These successive misfortunes did not affect Gauguin's determination. His work, as much as his obstinate pursuit of experience, proved to his friends that, from now on, he was exclusively a painter, ready to face the rigorous conditions of the period in order to find freer expression. He took part in the eighth Impressionist exhibition in the rue

22

THE ALYSCAMPS (1888) ❯
LOUVRE, PARIS

Laffitte, showing a group of paintings of which Felix Fénéon wrote: "Paul Gauguin's colours have a limited range, giving his pictures a dull harmony." This simple sentence shows how far detached from Impressionism he had already become, how he was less interested in the sparkle of light and the instability of nature than in discovering its basic immutability, in fact its essence. Departing from the realism of the Impressionists he was already abandoning their technique to discover a more lasting, more durable form of expression.

He was not satisfied with an analytical approach and drifted, probably unwittingly, towards a synthesis of which he was gradually to become aware. The detachment from Impressionism betrayed itself in his technique by a different use of colour, a stronger line, tighter composition and an acceptance of tonal contrasts not for the purpose of expressing the changeability of the atmosphere but to compose an individual rhythm for each picture.

Once more, material conditions seemed to react on his work. In an attempt to adapt his life to his very meagre income, he decided to live in Brittany, at Pont-Aven.

At the Pension Gloanec he was able in that city to exist on a very modest expenditure. He may not have been attracted to Brittany purely for financial reasons. Charles Morice who knew him well has given another reason: "sadness". But this does not seem convincing, for, on the contrary, his passionate nature had to expand and what has been called a taste for sadness which he found in Brittany seems to have been a desire for concentration, a mysticism that corresponded to his own inclinations. Daniel de Monfreid claims that Gauguin went to discover "an atmosphere and environment different from our ultra-civilized milieu, so that, in his works, he could return to primitive art".

All these reactions and feelings are more clearly express-ed in the commentaries of Gauguin's friends than in his work. He may have been rediscovering the primitive, but this did not appear in his pictures. In no way did they reveal particularly careful composition, and the first signs of this were to appear a few years later. We may suppose, then, that he was attracted to Brittany mainly by chance and the opportunity to live somewhere cheaply, but he discovered places and things to which he became at tached, finding that they agreed with his own instinct and quickly making use of them. It is quite likely that he would have found what he was unconsciously looking for in Provence or Spain just as well as in Brittany. Gauguin carried his dream within him and it was revealed at the right moment. Outward circumstances were no more than a pretext. The most one can say is that the charm of the Ile de France with the subtle light that had meant so much to the Impressionists was completely opposed to Gauguin's budding aesthetics. Though the sober forms and stiff horizons of Brittany may have given him pleasure the colours probably did not altogether suit his taste. He may have been satisfied with the "dull harmonies" and "limited range of colours" mentioned by Fénéon, but they were probably not enough for him. His instinctive

SELF PORTRAIT DEDICATED TO VINCENT (VAN GOGH) (1888)
W. VAN GOGH COLLECTION, LAAREN

lyricism was ill at ease there; for him gravity did not exclude
passion any more than moderation forbade intensity. Such
sentiments still appear contradictory in so far as he had
not yet found the way to combine them according to a
personal formula.

He was also probably beginning to understand that an artist has the right to invent his entire vocabulary, accepting nature as his point of departure while subduing it to a discipline imposed by himself.

STILL-LIFE (FÊTE GLOANEC) (1888)
FORMERLY COLLECTION MAURICE DENIS

V

Tempted by the Exotic

Martinique (1887)

At this point memories of childhood and visions left him by his stay in Peru crowded Gauguin's mind. Sun and lively colours lent the exotic scene an irreplaceable attraction. With such a light, with such intense tones, there could be no place for misfortune or melancholy. Whether or not it was sadness that attracted Gauguin to Brittany, it proved a partial reason for him to leave, impelling him to lands beyond the seas where he believed that gaiety formed part of everyday life.

This vision haunted his dreams so intensely that he made up his mind to go abroad and embarked for Panama with his friend, Laval. He was, however, dogged by poverty which hampered all his acts and decisions, bringing even his most modest hopes to nothing.

He still had to live from day to day in exhausting conditions and in Panama he obtained employment among the labourers digging the Canal. Despite sickness and miserable wages he succeeded after a few months in getting to Martinique. There his work expressed something approaching joy; at any rate, he gave the impression that he was nearing discovery of himself. He probably felt in tune with the luxuriant vegetation, the intense blue of the sea, the blazing sky, the primitive inhabitants with their graceful unaffected attitudes, and the huge trees twined with creepers, raising their high, frail trunks into the air like a pattern of columns. He was not tempted to look at Martinique with the eyes of an Impressionist, nor was he specially attracted by the picturesqueness of the inhabitants and their way of life. Faced with the exuberance of nature he seemed to be drawn by something deeper, almost austere. Even in a landscape that he clearly portrayed according to nature, he successfully imparts a rigidity that defines its structure, retaining what is essential and discarding the superfluous. He was certainly stimulated by the exotic but, above all, he found it a confirmation of his temperament, a reflection of his power and recently regained freedom. This enabled him to introduce into his pictures the idea of a strictly personal rhythm, a kind of spatial geometry or construction, dominated by vertical lines in which each figure and object takes on a well-defined shape, forming part of a general composition which, though venturesome, proclaims an exactitude within spontaneous creativity.

We must compare the canvases which he brought back from Martinique with those of the Impressionists of the same period in order to understand the distance travelled by Gauguin in so short a time. He had unconsciously become opposed to the influences which had formed him and which he had admired. His new style is far closer to Cézanne than to Renoir or Monet and in many of the pictures of this period may be noted the technique of strong hatching so characteristic of the former artist. Gauguin made use of this in such a way that his work never gives any feeling of similarity or plagiarism.

During this period his forms begin to take on density. They no longer melt into the atmosphere as in the work of Monet but are surrounded by a circle forming a colour boundary, giving each figure or tree trunk its definite place in the composition. Within the limits imposed by his draughtsmanship with its intentional formalism, his use of colour is fluid and fragmentary, glowing with strongly opposed contrasts rather than with dots applied to the surface. It was not enough for figures and objects merely to occupy an exact space in his pictures; he attempted to render them in relief. The exotic was not a means of evading the issue with picturesque embroideries. It was a means of coming to harsher grips with nature, discovering its rhythms and uniting it with a feeling for the Classicism so despised by the Impressionists. This unconscious return to Classicism is one of the most notable characteristics of Gauguin's later work.

◀ BRETON CHILDREN AT THE SEASIDE (1889)
  PRINCE MATSUKATA COLLECTION

THE SCHUFFENECKER FAMILY (1889)
PRINCE MATSUKATA COLLECTION

VI

Synthetism and Symbolism
Brittany, Arles (1888)

Gauguin had to resume his wandering life, despite the beneficial effects of work and the lessons learnt in Martinique. Once more he was harrassed by sickness and poverty. Worn out by dysentery he came back to Paris where he received a friendly welcome from Schuffenecker who had also left the Bourse to devote himself to painting. He gave Gauguin shelter in the studio which he owned in the rue Boulard. In the spring of 1888 Gauguin returned to Brittany where he found his friend, Laval, another young painter named Emile Bernard whom he had already met during a previous stay, and Paul Serusier who, a few months later, was to make Gauguin's name known to the students of the Académie Julian.

In the course of a few years his ideas had become so mature that they needed only expression, and it was at this point that the theories of synthetism linked to symbolism came into being. Frequent attempts have been made to discover who first invented the simplified draughtsmanship expressive of symbolism and, in particular, the bands, usually blue, that surrounded forms. It has already been noted that traces of these can be found in the canvases executed by Gauguin in Martinique in 1887. The systematic adoption of the formula seems to have been due to the initiative of Emile Bernard who showed Gauguin the results of his investigations in 1888, interesting him so much in them that Gauguin took to making use of the discoveries in his own work. There is no longer any doubt about this order of events and it is accepted by the majority of art historians. In fact the formula was no more than a means to an end for Gauguin; no recipe can ever give genius to those who do not already possess it. Symbolism was suggested to Gauguin

33

BRETON LANDSCAPE (1889)
BUHRLE COLLECTION, ZURICH

at a very advantageous moment, and seemed to him a conclusion to the experiments he had recently carried out during his journey to Martinique.

This conception of painting, in which each form is allotted the strictest boundaries, has an inevitable reaction on colour. There is no longer any basic need or reason for it to be dispersed in small strokes; it is no longer necessary to obtain general unity by causing the entire surface of the picture to flicker with light; each zone of colour and each section of the composition may be organized to contrast with the rest, each piece having its own unity and harmony with the whole. Hence the necessity for the revival of large areas of colour and the abolition of tonal divisions.

Having reached this stage, Gauguin was in entire possession of style and technique. His later works were to show no appreciable advance, apart from greater freedom and mastery. It is possible, however, that he still had doubts about acknowledging such a complete change of technique. Proof of this lies in a still-life executed for Mme. Gloanec's birthday in 1888 which in its design, draughtsmanship and colour could well pass as a work of the Tahiti period. Feeling that this composition was outrageously revolutionary, Gauguin did not dare to inscribe it with his own name, and modestly signed it "Madeleine B." (Madeleine Bernard, sister of Emile) in the hope that it would be accepted.

One more event was to convince him of the validity of his new technique, allowing him then an irrevocable detachment and greater boldness (for which his contemporaries did not thank him, and which certainly did not improve his material situation). After his return from Martinique his health continued to be poor. Van Gogh had just begun to live at Arles and insisted that Gauguin should join him there. Many surviving letters reveal Van Gogh's friendly overtures and Gauguin's grumbling hesitation, but at last he let himself be persuaded and arrived in Provence at the end of October. Despite their mutual admiration the two men could not live together. Their passions were opposed and, although they were as one regarding their creative plans, they came to blows over the trivialities of daily life.

Van Gogh's mind was disturbed by too many failures, too much pride, and too long periods of hopeful waiting. One December evening he completely lost control of himself and attacked Gauguin with a razor. No injury was done then, but Van Gogh returned home and cut off an

STILL-LIFE WITH ONIONS AND JAPANESE ENGRAVING (1889)
PRIVATE COLLECTION, BASLE

STILL-LIFE WITH JAPANESE PRINT AND VASE (1889)
ITTLESON COLLECTION, NEW YORK

ear which he took to a prostitute. For some time after he
was in an asylum; Gauguin returned to Paris.

His stay in Provence had been very short; he arrived
on October 22nd, 1888 and was back in Paris at the beginning of 1889. These two months, however, saw the
end of many years of searching. The year 1888 with its
countless moves concluded Gauguin's attempts to reach
extreme simplicity. His circle of friends in Paris, the poets

he had met, his followers in Brittany, the passionate summons of Van Gogh, were all signs of a personality gaining strength, and dominating those around.

The school of Pont-Aven came into existence without any conscious wish on his part. Serusier who had met him there returned to Paris, bringing the news to his friends at the Académie Julian; they included Bonnard, Vuillard and Ranson. Gauguin started to collaborate with the ceramist Chaplet, executing some pottery and decorating it himself. The pieces were extremely original and Chaplet agreed to fire them. The canvases painted in Brittany and Martinique, together with the pottery, were exhibited at Boussod and Valadon.

1888 had begun with the return to disappointment from Martinique, had continued amid wretched financial circumstances, and ended with the tragic drama at Arles. The balance lay in Gauguin's expansion and the passionate activity through which he found corroboration of himself and saw his influence extend over others. If we set his achievements alongside his financial failure, it is clear how the artist's pride was satisfied and how he could scoff at material difficulties. Art had become an end in itself, assuming the dimensions of religion, especially as the artist's ideology agreed with that of the poets of his time.

Gauguin's synthetism answered the theories of poetic symbolism whose followers wrote in the new *Mercure de France*. The period favoured the elaboration of a system combining aesthetics with philosophy, and it attracted him for a time, giving an appearance of style to what was really the fulfilment of his own personality. However arbitrary the ideas he took as his basis, they gained him friends and followers who were to be invaluable to him in the struggle which henceforward was directed against the routines of academism and the now almost traditional audacities of the triumphant Impressionists.

There was no longer any question in Gauguin's mind of reproducing nature: it had to be recreated with the maximum intensity in order to express not material truth but the feelings experienced by the artist. He expressed this very clearly when he wrote to Schuffenecker: "Do not copy nature too much. Art is an abstraction: draw it out of nature in a dream when you are thinking more about the act of creation than the result." In the same strain, he advised Serusier to use the most vivid green if he was struck by the colour of a meadow and the deepest red for a stain which had caught his attention. From this can be seen his need to make sensations subject to ideas and the representation of reality to imagination. To obtain this maximum of intensity, however, Gauguin considered the small strokes of the Impressionists too fluid; one broad splash of colour is more powerful and effective than a lot of small ones side by side.

It was not, therefore, from a spirit of contradiction that Gauguin finally broke with the Impressionists, but because he was temperamentally dissatisfied with the photographic approach which pleased them so much. He did not wish to discover immediate sensation through nature but a deeper and more lasting feeling, a more durable passion, and the

TE FARE MAORIE: THE MAORI HOUSE (1891)
PRIVATE COLLECTION, RHEINFELDEN, SWITZERLAND

expression of grandeur pertaining more to a general rhythm than to casual aspects.

Following on Brittany, Arles brought him definite confirmation in his search and from now on he was to embark on his art with his conceptions totally renewed.

FARMYARD AT POULDU (1890) ❯
EMERY REVES COLLECTION

VII

Hope lies in the Antipodes, Madagascar or Tonkin

(1889–1891)

The division of Gauguin's life between Brittany and Paris is less evidence of his unstable character than of his continually baffled hopes of improving his situation and his disappointments in his contacts with his fellow men. Gauguin was a combination of prophet and hermit, and his dislike of mankind was often due to his open-hearted-

ness being repulsed. Nevertheless, we must not blame those who disappointed him for his failures. His stubborn pride irritated those who could have helped him and were better disposed towards him than he believed.

The future was to confirm that Gauguin was usually misunderstood because his behaviour could not be judged by ordinary standards; all his actions were in accordance with his nature and were seldom within the boundaries of accepted convention. It was this inability to compromise that was partly responsible for the attraction he exercised on some of the very original writers and painters of a period, apparently centred round *Mercure de France*, particularly rich in originality. Jarry, Verlaine, Léon Bloy, Van Gogh, Gauguin, to name only the most famous, provide a range of disconcerting, strangely compelling figures.

1889 was the year of the Exposition Universelle, a year which saw the Eiffel Tower rise from the Champ de Mars and faith pledged in the conquering powers of industry and universal science. Hopes were centred on a better world in which spiritual forces would strive for agreement with the powerful materialism about to create a new order. Artists found this still imperfect world difficult to accept. Anarchy tempted them as much as solitude. They required a fresh set of symbols in an attempt to retain the old order as much as to interpret and spiritualise the new.

Gauguin could not resist playing a part in this passionate atmosphere where café conversations outlined philosophical systems and new religions. Nietzsche, Péladan and the Rose-Croix group found as many supporters among

TAHITIAN WOMEN (1891)
LOUVRE, PARIS

painters. The school of Pont-Aven reformed around Gauguin who had returned to Brittany, taking up new quarters in an inn at Le Pouldu.

The atmosphere of enthusiasm and revolt allowed him to carry his boldness to its limits. Breaking free from the fetters of the past, he experimented whole-heartedly with his newly adopted formula of large zones of colour ringed

43

by a firm line. During the Exposition Universelle, he organized a show with his friends in the nearby Café Volpini where under the banner of synthetism could be found Emile Bernard, Louis Anquetin, Charles Laval, Schuffenecker, Louis Roy, Léon Fouché, Georges Daniel and Ludovic Némo. Together with Emile Bernard he published an album of lithographs for which Brittany, Martinique and Arles provided subjects in the same style. At Pont-Aven, Laval, Filiger, Meyer de Haan, Seguin and Verkade listened to their master and embarked on a new aesthetic known as *cloisonnisme*. Their works and wild way of life shocked the artists of milder character who also came to Brittany in search of peace and a cheaper existence.

Gauguin walked round the countryside, setting up his easel in front of different types of landscape, always with the desire of surpassing nature so as to attain wider simplifications. In the church at Trémalo a rustic Calvary showed him the emotion and sincerity inherent in the simplicity of peasant art. In his painting of it he tried to rediscover the equivalent of this unsophisticated boldness. The result was a masterpiece, the famous picture called *The Yellow Christ*. His work during this period shocked everyone and his hotel-keeper refused to accept a portrait of herself now in the Louvre under the title of *La belle Angèle*.

Scandal and lack of understanding were just as virulent in Paris, but Gauguin's reputation continued to rise among the coteries, and he had frequent meetings with the writers at the Café Voltaire. Albert Aurier was an ardent supporter of pictorial synthetism which complemented poetic symbolism and, among the friends Gauguin met, were Moréas, Verlaine and Charles Morice. He willingly played the part of head of a school of painting, sometimes affecting an originality bordering on the eccentric. But basically the atmosphere did not suit him; affectation was not in his nature.

He had an ever more overwhelming need for solitude which was one of the chief incentives for his stay in Brittany. He felt a desire to escape the civilized world, a desire similar to that which had led to his journey to Martinique. Once more he dreamed of the legendary exoticism of unknown lands. In letters to his friends he conjured up possibilities of escape to Madagascar or Tonkin, envisaging the ideal form of life that could be lived there, carefully calculating the cost, and suggesting that he might obtain reductions from the government for the journey. He tried to persuade his friends to join in his dreams, sketching a magnificent plan for a "studio in the tropics"; together they would discover a sunny Eden where they could paint in complete freedom with no material cares apart from gathering the fruits with which nature would generously supply them.

The illusion had a seemingly logical basis, an accumulation of documented facts which Gauguin took seriously and which apparently for the time being convinced his friends. Emile Bernard, Meyer de Haan and Laval all supported his hallucinations. But when it became a question of practical details, when the project really took shape and the departure was definitely fixed, Gauguin had no supporters. He decided to leave France in a lone attempt to start life again in the Antipodes, a life which would be happier, simpler and more intense.

His final choice was Tahiti, but again he did not succeed in getting any of his friends to share in the adventure. A great sale was organized in support of the project. Octave Mirbeau wrote an article about it in the *Echo de Paris* of February 16th, 1891; it was intended to be a preface to the catalogue, attracting the attention of col-

TA MATETE: THE MARKET (1892)
BASLE MUSEUM, SWITZERLAND

lectors with the case of "a man fleeing from civilization, voluntarily seeking silence and oblivion in order to become more conscious of himself and better able to hear those inner voices which are stifled in the uproar of our passions and disputes".

The sale consisted of thirty pictures; it brought in the sum of 9,860 francs. To celebrate Gauguin's departure, his friends gathered at the Café Voltaire on March 23rd for a great banquet. Amongst those present were Rachilde, Eugène Carrière, Odilon Redon, Jean Dolent, Charles Morice, Jean Moréas, Albert Aurier, Saint-Pol Roux, Julien Leclercq, Adolphe Rette, Edouard Dubus, Dauphin Meunier and Alfred Vallette.

Shortly afterwards, the tribute to Gauguin was completed by an evening performance given by the *Théâtre d'Art* at the Vaudeville. The profits were to be divided between the artist and Paul Verlaine. This friendly celebration was held in May, but there were no profits, and Gauguin was unable to be present. On April 4th his friends saw him off from the Gare de Lyon for Marseilles and Tahiti.

VIII

Noa-Noa and the First Stay in Tahiti
(1891–1893)

Before leaving Paris, Gauguin took steps to make his establishment in Tahiti easier. As the result of overtures made by his friends he succeeded in being entrusted with

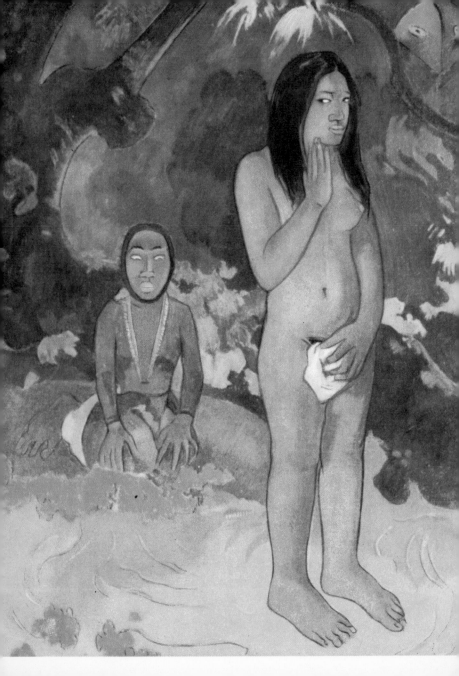

an official mission by the Ministry for the Colonies "to study the customs and landscape of the country". The

WHAT! ARE YOU JEALOUS? (1892)
HERMITAGE MUSEUM, LENINGRAD

appointment was unpaid but was bound to facilitate his connections with the local authorities.

His arrival, however, caused the authorities some surprise. He appeared rather oddly dressed, his long hair

◀ PARAU NA TE VARUA INO: THE DEVIL'S WORDS (1892)
MR. & MRS. AVERELL HARRIMAN COLLECTION, NEW YORK

hanging down over his shoulders, giving him the look of an exhausted Christ, very unlike a civil servant's idea of someone charged with a semi-official mission to a colony. From the start it was possible to feel the lack of contact between the Europeans already there and the newly arrived Gauguin. He was naturally hostile to this society and was ready to play the part of the new-born savage in front of its petty tyrants.

"Here," he said, "was the Europe from which I had thought to escape, masquerading under the irritating form of colonial snobbery, childish imitation, grotesque to the point of caricature. That was not what I had come so far to seek."

He felt his dream dissolving around him. Shortly after his arrival on June 8th, King Pomare V died. "With him vanished the last traces of the customs and grandeur of the past. The Maori tradition was dead and finished. Civilization had triumphed with its soldiery, businessmen and civil servants."

Gauguin's one aim was to get away. He left Papeete for the interior in an attempt to find closer contact with the natives, to share their way of life, to know their gods, their joys and anxieties. In spite of disappointments it seems from the evidence of a manuscript called *Noa-noa* in which he described his life at this time, that he had some vivid experiences there. He relates the colourful details of his new life, telling how he first acquired a hut and then a companion; it was a simple existence, the days filled with work, the nights haunted by the spirits of Maori gods.

Gauguin very soon felt at ease in this world where he found more or less what he had been waiting for. "I have all the joys of a free existence, animal and human. I have escaped from the artificial into the natural world. With the certainty of a tomorrow as free and beautiful as today, peace descends on me. I develop naturally and have no more vain cares."

His art profited not so much from subject inspiration as from a confirmation of the freedom he had already achieved in France. From now on he was aware that, for him, structure was the primary requirement in a work of art, just as emotions and uncomplicated actions were the basis of his daily life.

It is true that he devoted himself exclusively to local themes but there is no fundamental difference between his heroes in Tahiti and *The Yellow Christ*, and his still-lifes with their exotic fruits are very similar to the one he presented to Mme. Gloanec. The most one can say is that his figures are more majestic and show greater freedom from restraint. Their naked bodies are more in accordance with nature than those of his Breton women and, for this reason, their poses acquire authentic grandeur. Their grace is completely devoid of mannerism, lying as it does in the generous scale of the figures and a sculptural fullness which gives Gauguin's art its real significance. It is comparable to the art of the great mural painters and, even in the smallest canvases, avoids the trifling charm of easel painting. Where his admired friend Puvis de Chavannes found elegance, he finds grandeur. His abundant

THE SIESTA (1893)
IRA HAUPT COLLECTION, NEW YORK

forms move in space so coloured that one gets no impression of emptiness in the canvas, nor, on the other hand, is it constricted by too compact an atmosphere. There are no voids in his compositions, no gaps between the individual elements, but none the less the air circulates.

Gauguin's art now attained a fullness and serenity hitherto unknown to him; it is probably unexampled in

52

OTAHI: ALONE (1893)
MME. O. SAINSÈRE COLLECTION, PARIS

French painting since the seventeenth century, when Poussin's art embodied the greatest sense of order for a civilized society. Under the pretext of drawing his inspiration from a primitive people, Gauguin rediscovered the great tradition of classicism, thus banishing every trace of his connection with the Impressionists.

Gauguin's art at this stage is wholly his own invention but, paradoxically, some of his canvases do not appear really revolutionary until one studies them in detail. At a first glance they seem directly inspired by nature and a faithful reproduction of it. Closer examination is needed to reveal the considerable contribution of the artist. Then one notices that a tree is blue, a banana red, a path green, and a meadow pink. None of the colours correspond with reality but the relations between them are so strictly and

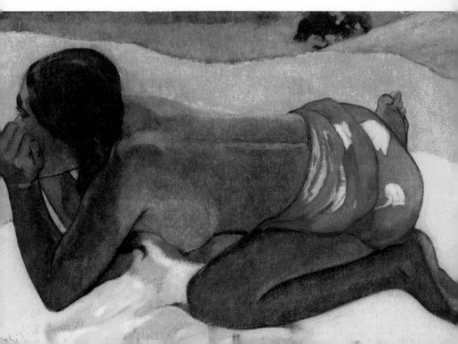

accurately observed that one does not immediately become aware of the contradictions. Only careful analysis reveals the violence of Gauguin's invention. At this period he achieved definite, total expression of himself, creating an art of his very own, every element of which he constructed himself. It was a perfectly lucid, conscious form which asked no more of nature than to provide an initial suggestion.

This perfection was no doubt developed during the preceding years. Gauguin's visits to Brittany, Martinique and Provence each contributed a share to his discovery of a new world of expression, and we may rightly surmise that when he arrived in Tahiti he was already in full possession of the style and technique that was from now on to be characteristic of his work. It remains none the less true, however, that he found in Tahiti the climate in which his art could expand and strengthen.

In order to understand the intimate harmony existing between the man and the country, one should read what he wrote in *Noa-noa* about his adventures, impressions and enthusiasms. A few years later he entrusted its publication to his friend, Charles Morice, and it first appeared in the *Editions de la Plume*. After his death it came out in a facsimile edition containing several notable differences from the printed text. Finally Le Garrec published the original text in facsimile in which can be seen important variations from the version of Charles Morice. However this may be, *Noa-noa* shows Gauguin in complete harmony with the customs of the country, moved by its

MILL IN BRITTANY (1894)
PRINCE MATSUKATA COLLECTION

legends, attracted by its gods, and drawn towards its
people. He seemed to have gained balance and found
spiritual well being – he was happy.

In fact, the truth is not so simple. Gauguin's happiness
was not so complete and his life less serene than *Noa-noa*
would have us believe. There are other texts to prove the

reverse. His letters to his friend, Daniel de Monfreid, in particular, reveal his desperate anxieties. He was constantly worried about money; he suffered from ill health and interfering administrators.

In March he wrote: "I have been seriously ill. Such spittings of blood, a quarter of a litre a day. Quite impossible to stop it; mustard plasters on the legs, cupping-glasses on the chest, neither any good. The hospital doctor was very anxious and thought I was done for." In November came another complaint: "My health is bad. Not that I am ill (the climate is wonderful) but all these anxieties over money do me no good, and I have suddenly aged a good deal in an astonishing way. Besides, I don't eat in order to face the state of my affairs and carry on in spite of it. Only a little bread and tea, which makes me lose weight and strength and spoils my stomach."

Faced with so many difficulties, he thought of returning. In June 1892 he wrote to Daniel de Monfreid: I have been to the town 40 kilometres away to see the Governor and try to get a passage for France." The archives of the Ministry for the Colonies preserves these requests. Their offices had not made allowances in their budgets for this type of expense and the matter was passed from one to the other. The Paris offices had no funds for such things. Gauguin felt the need to return to France to put his affairs in order, for he knew quite well that his work was more and more attracting the attention of collectors. At last his applications met with success and he arrived in France on August 5th, 1893.

SELF-PORTRAIT KNOWN AS "AU GOLGOTHA" (1896)
SÃO PAOLO MUSEUM, BRAZIL

IX

The Attempt to Return
Paris, Brittany (1893–1895)

Gauguin disembarked at Marseilles with four francs in his pocket. His first letter was clearly a call for help to enable him to leave there and reach Paris. Poverty continued to harrass him. The tragedy of his life lay not only in this grasping penury, but also in the sudden changes of circumstances which would transform an utterly desperate situation at the most unforeseen moment. At the beginning of September one of his uncles who lived at Orléans died, leaving Gauguin the sum of 13,000 francs, quite a considerable amount at this time. He made use of it to organize an exhibition of his recent works at Durand-Ruel which resulted in financial loss but excited lively curiosity. The catalogue reveals that it contained an amazing collection, bringing together several masterpieces which are now the pride of museums outside France. *Ia Orana Maria, Once Upon a Time, Festival of Hiva, Why are you Angry? The Seed of the Areois* and *Woman with a Mango* magnificently summed up his work in Tahiti. Of the forty pictures and two sculptures exhibited only eleven attracted purchasers and Gauguin again found himself in conflict with the intractable, almost hostile indifference of Paris.

He took up his quarters in a picturesque studio in the rue Vercingétorix where he tried, beneath the skies of Paris, to reconstitute the atmosphere of his exotic life. In

a desire to be original he dressed eccentrically in a long blue frock-coat with mother-of-pearl buttons; a blue shirt, buttoning at the side, with a border of yellow and green embroidery, putty-coloured trousers; a grey hat with a sky-blue ribbon, and white gloves. The originality of his clothes matched his domestic life which he shared with a coloured girl, known as Annah the Javanese, whom he had discovered in Montmartre. But it was not enough to

59

satisfy him, and he left Paris in 1894, first for a brief stay in Belgium and then for a futile meeting with his wife in Copenhagen, after which he returned to Brittany in the spring, staying at Le Pouldu and Pont-Aven.

His journeys, his instability, his almost feverish outward activity and the disappointments he experienced as the result of his exhibition and his attempt to re-establish relations with his family, are all proof at least of his well-intentioned efforts to take up normal contacts again with the civilized world. But they also show that it was impossible for him to adapt himself to a conventional existence. The mental images of Tahiti were too powerful and too highly coloured to be erased by his present way of life. They could not be supplanted; even in Brittany he painted pictures representing Tahitian scenes. He preferred his memories to what he actually saw, and perhaps his representing such scenes was a way of ridding himself of the hold they had over him. He made attempts to adapt the breadth of his new vision to the Breton landscape.

Gauguin seemed more and more a misfit. One day, during a walk at Concarneau, an argument broke out between him and a group of sailors who were making fun of Annah. It ended in a fight in which one of Gauguin's assailants kicked him with his sabot and broke his ankle. He was carried off on a stretcher and never recovered from his injury. On his return to Paris he found that Annah, who had gone back before him, had disappeared, taking with her everything that attracted her in the studio.

All this proved to Gauguin that his place was really not in France. The friendships on which he relied were too exceptional and too few to justify his presence and hold him away from lands where he had found a balance better suited to his nature. He saw nothing for it but a fresh departure and, as on the first occasion, decided to hold a sale to obtain the money needed for his journey.

From the poet and dramatist, August Strindberg, he received a letter to serve as preface to the catalogue of the sale which took place at the Hotel Drouot on February 18th, 1895. It resulted in a failure, most of the works being bought back by Gauguin himself. Only one picture fetched 900 francs, and none of the others brought more than 500. He had had all his luck. His departure was unheralded and there was no banquet.

We may wonder what feelings he experienced during this final crossing. Maybe the sadness and bitterness of the exile, abandoning or abandoned by his family, little missed by his friends, almost a laughing stock in his own country. Or possibly the joyful anticipation and eager hopes of one regaining a peaceful haven, a brightly coloured dreamland, a life of silence and simplicity.

Until now every stage of Gauguin's life had played a significant part in the development of his art, but his last stay in France appears quite superfluous apart from marking total rebellion, shattering the last of his illusions, and enabling him to make a final break without any feeling of regret. Gauguin stepped aside from the western world, and it is only fair to say that this world rejected him each time he tried to reintegrate himself or come to some terms with it. The tragedy of his life is that we can both make him responsible for his failures and see them as the in-

NEVERMORE (1897)
COURTAULD INSTITUTE OF ART, LONDON

struments of his destiny. It is impossible to decide whether he was the plaything or the originator of his misfortunes, and in this lies the grandeur of the drama.

MATERNITY (1896)
PRIVATE COLLECTION, NEW YORK

X
Final Departure — Who are We?
Tahiti (1895–1897)

Gauguin's renewed contact with the exotic was not as easy nor as beneficial from a material point of view as he could have hoped. Signs of alternate hope and despair appear in all his letters. He finally wrote: "I am not only at the end of my resources, but at the end of my strength. Everything is exhausted and my will is now very weak."

Calls for help increased. In Paris, his loyal friend, Daniel de Monfreid, went to endless expense to find collectors and make a few successful sales on his behalf. In the calm of a primitive life Gauguin's needs were few. "I am not unreasonable," he wrote, "I and my *vahine*, a young girl of thirteen and a half, live on 100 francs a month; you see that is not much; on top of that my tobacco, soap, and a dress for the girl come to 10 francs a month. And you should see where I live! There are two coconut tree trunks carved in the form of Kanaka gods; arbutus in flower, a little shed for the carriage and a horse."

Despite this modest expenditure, Gauguin had not come to the end of his difficulties. His health grew worse, and whenever it seemed to improve, his financial problems became more pressing. A cruel cycle of illness and defaulting creditors continually made life almost impossible for him and prevented him from getting any rest.

Meanwhile his work was gaining in grandeur and serenity. His despair appears in several of his pictures, but it has no material form, and is more or less a caricature of material poverty and the degradation of man. His characters are obsessed and haunted by deep, secret forces. The eyes of his women are turned inward as if contemplating phantoms or awaiting in silent despair the decisions of their gods; his motionless models have the quality of an incantation. They seem to be at prayer, in the service of a mystery belonging to some secret world. Gauguin shares in the exotic magic: at first he was only a spectator but now he seems to have fully grasped it. This being so, there is nothing astonishing in the fact that the figures in some of his compositions surpass the simple human scale. They have a breadth and majesty that makes them symbols of a semi-divine nature.

Sometimes, however, Gauguin relaxed, executing more familiar scenes tinged with irony, portraying native women gossiping over their everyday tasks. He makes us share their simple existence, giving the impression that he is not an indifferent spectator, but has completely adopted his characters' way of life. If his work expresses both simple happiness and grandeur, it is because, as an artist, he wished to ignore the difficulties of mankind, and tried to create, ignoring the disappointments that continued to overwhelm him. Illness and lack of money are recurrent themes in his correspondence, and it is possible to note strange contradictions between his conditions of life and his work. Their reconciliation assumes a dramatic character; Gauguin appears greater for having suffered so much without letting any sign of it appear in his canvases.

In several letters he wrote: "I am not only at the end of my resources, but at the end of my strength . . . Since my arrival my health has grown daily worse, my injured foot gives me a great deal of pain and I have two wounds that the doctor cannot get to mend . . . To-day I am prostrate, half exhausted by the thankless struggle on which I have embarked, I am on my knees and put aside all my pride. I am nothing, only a failure . . . My precarious situation becomes more and more intolerable."

He picked up courage with improved health: "I am beginning to get better and have profited by it to put up a greater fight." Sometimes things seemed to be about to take a more normal course. At the beginning of 1897 he wrote: "Here I am then, my debts paid, out of danger for six to eight months." But, as always, these were only temporary alleviations.

He had just learnt of the death of his daughter, Aline, the child he had considered most like himself. He had thought that she would be able to understand him, and had composed a moving note-book for her with the dedication: "For my daughter when she is twenty". On receiving the news he wrote to his friend, Daniel de Monfreid: "I am in utter despair. Somewhere up there I obviously have a friend who doesn't give me a moment's peace." A few months later he wrote to his wife: "I have just lost my daughter, I no longer love God. She was called Aline like my mother. Her tomb over there with its flowers is all illusion. Her tomb is here near me; my tears are those living flowers." Mette Gauguin never ans-

67

wered this letter and from now on their correspondence ceased.

All Gauguin's plans had failed, all promises dispersed, all hopes were disappointed. It is possible he had the feeling that, as an artist, he had achieved a form of total self-expression in which he had rediscovered the grandeur of classicism and which at the same time contained a mystic world, the apotheosis of paganism, entirely suitable to the way of life he witnessed every day. To confirm that

NAVE NAVE MAHANA: DELIGHTFUL DAYS (1896)
LYON MUSEUM

TAHITIAN LANDSCAPE (1901)
BUHRLE COLLECTION, ZURICH

he was at the centre of the mystery, was clearly conscious of it, and that his art was wholly impregnated with the harmony of forms and thoughts, he executed a large canvas which he called: *Whence do we come? What are we? Where are we going?* The symbolism is complex and inclined to be unintelligible at first sight. Its greatness lies not so much in its narrative value or in the literary significance of the symbolism, as in its breadth of composition, rich colours, resonant harmonies and poetic feeling. In it is summed up Gauguin's entire output of the preceding years. His previous canvases were no more than preparatory studies for this spacious, decorative and unusually proportioned piece. It simultaneously expresses serenity and despair, mingling idols and human beings.

This was Gauguin's testament and his final creative work.

At the beginning of 1898, he tried to poison himself, but the dose of arsenic which he took was too strong and brought on vomiting which got rid of the poison. He exchanged death for hideous suffering. Completed during the last weeks of 1897, Gauguin dated the great composition 1898 to show that it marked a final point. "I wished before my death to paint the great canvas that I had in mind, and, throughout the month, I worked day and night in an unprecedented fever."

Gauguin would have terminated his life at this point, if he had been master of his own destiny, but it was not to be. Once again he escaped the desired consequences of his actions and continued his painful way.

XI

The Man Finds Fulfilment
Tahiti, La Dominique (1893–1903)

After the failure of his suicide, Gauguin began life again with the same expectations and the same disappointments but, despite appearances, he was not the same man. The

SUNFLOWERS ON A CHAIR (1901)
BUHRLE COLLECTION, ZURICH

tone of his letters scarcely changed and his correspondence still consisted of constant calls for help and continual claims against his creditors. He also kept on instructing his friend, Daniel de Monfreid, to keep an eye on his threatened interests in France.

In the domain of his inward self, however, we can perceive a considerable change, indicative that, from this time on, his mental condition had altered. His work was now noticeably different from that of the previous years. His suicide attempt and the great canvas preceding it marked a final point at least in one series of events.

Gauguin no longer felt that he could turn back and, if he did still sometimes think of returning to Europe, he regarded it as a mental illusion, not seriously supported by his real self. From now on his art expressed the certainty and unreserved agreement of the savage he had become, a standpoint which was not going to make life easy for him.

He immersed himself more deeply in native life. His work was enriched by this; mentally he benefited, but materially things grew worse because civilized man, whatever he does, is branded by civilization and cannot overcome the variance between it and primitive life. Even when adopted by the natives, it is impossible to prevent the semi-civilized from regarding a compatriot whose thoughts and acts are in such harsh contradiction to theirs, with suspicion and malice. They considered Gauguin a kind of traitor because he took sides with the natives against them. A feeling of unrestricted justice and morality was set against class morality; conflict was inevitable.

All Gauguin's attempts to come to an agreement with his fellow countrymen were doomed to failure. He accepted a job in a Government Office, but only went there reluctantly with the idea that what he was doing was a humiliating concession. Regarding this he wrote: "I am going to drink my shame, and God knows how I shall do the work required of me by an artilleryman . . . they won't be able to say that I have neglected my duty."

He gave up the post, but his quarrels with the administration did not improve. He believed himself the object of persecution, and, no doubt, the civil servants really were intolerant of this hostile, rule-breaking renegade. Gauguin was not sparing of his attacks, publishing violent polemics in the newspaper, *Les Guêpes*. The magistrate who was the object of them was wise enough not to reply, which made Gauguin still more furious. "It resulted in nothing against myself," he wrote, "no duel, no proceedings: what rottenness in our colonies."

To uphold his claims, he decided to publish a paper of his own. This resulted in the publication of *Le Sourire*, handwritten by Gauguin and illustrated with his woodcuts. In it he continued to express his grievances and accusations which could only further embitter his relations with his fellow Europeans.

At last, worn out by so many annoyances, he thought of leaving the island which had become so inhospitable. "I shall go and settle on one of the Marquesas Islands where life is very easy and very cheap," he wrote. And in July 1901, he wrote to Charles Morice: "I am making a last effort by going to settle, next month, on Fatu-Iva, one of the Marquesas Islands whose inhabitants are still almost

STILL-LIFE WITH KNIFE (1901)
PRIVATE COLLECTION, SWITZERLAND

cannibals. I believe that there, the completely savage element and absolute solitude will before my death lead to a final blaze of enthusiasm which will rejuvenate my imagination and result in the conclusion of my talent."

Gauguin was not aware that he had achieved the summit and that, for several years past, each of his works had been sufficiently accomplished to form in itself the conclusion he always hoped to attain.

In Europe his talents had successfully attracted more and more experts. The dealer, Ambroise Vollard, became interested, drew up an agreement with him, and regularly bought his works, bringing him to the notice of a wider public. This improved state of affairs did not, however, bring Gauguin the peace he hoped for, though given even better circumstances, his nature would probably have prevented him from attaining it. He himself had often admitted that money slipped through his fingers and that, despite the best intentions, he always made the wrong decisions.

LANDSCAPE IN THE ISLANDS (1901)
HAHNLOSER COLLECTION, BERNE

In November 1901, he settled in Atuana, the chief village of La Dominique in the Marquesas. He built a hut roofed with leaves, its walls fashioned of plaited bamboo, in the centre of the village; it consisted of a huge studio with a small sleeping corner. Gauguin decorated it with pagan sculptures which the Europeans would have been only too ready to call licentious and, in this dwelling which he christened "The House of Carnal Pleasure", he resumed the warring life of a savage. The usual results followed and he found himself in constant conflict, either with the representatives of the Catholic Mission, or with the *gendarmes*.

He exerted himself more and more to help the natives against the Europeans, going so far as discouraging them from sending their children to school. His relations with the Catholic Mission grew steadily more bitter. He lodged a complaint against the *gendarme* in charge of the district who, in all probability, did not administer justice fairly. This charge called for a reply. Gauguin was prosecuted for defamation of character, lost his case, was fined 1,000 francs and condemned to three months imprisonment.

He wrote a manuscript with the title *Avant et après*, a kind of spiritual testament and balance-sheet corresponding to what *Whence do we come? What are we? Where are we going?* represented in his painting. In it he summed up his memories, his philosophy and aesthetics, his enthusiasms and aversions. His attempt to have it published was unsuccessful. He demanded payment of his income from France, but received it only irregularly.

His work at this period was strangely untroubled, but never superficial. A good example is the canvas called *The Sorcerer* in which he portrayed a somewhat mysterious character. In all his other works he gained access to a world removed from reality where the devils of despair had no further power. In short, there was no more room in his life or work for worries and anxiety. If misfortune struck him, it was outside himself, and no longer encroached upon his spiritual and aesthetic world which, from now on, was perfectly balanced.

Just when he had given such a clear impression of his fulfilment, his ordeals multiplied, but he would not admit defeat. Nevertheless, his sentence was a terrible blow: "I have just been caught in a dreadful trap," he wrote in April 1903. "It means my ruin and the complete destruction of my health." However, despite the letters in which he showed his despondency, he did not accept failure. Certain that he was in the right, he appealed, but he had no time left to wait for restitution of justice. On the morning of May 8th his native servant found him dead in bed; when his neighbour, Pastor Vernier, arrived, he could only record that "one leg hung out of the bed, still warm".

Order was completely restored. The Catholic Mission took possession of Gauguin's body and buried it according to the rites of the Church. The local authorities seized his surviving possessions and put them up for auction. His family became the heirs of a father they scarcely knew. His last paintings in his hut were auctioned, and his effects were scattered amid the mocking villagers.

TAHITIAN LANDSCAPE (1899–1902)
MRS. ARTHUR LEHMAN COLLECTION

Now the legend started, the mirage took shape. At the sale, a young naval officer named Victor Segalen devoutly bought Gauguin's palette along with a few of his drawings and a canvas which, paradoxically enough in this sunny land, represented a Breton landscape under snow. Back in Paris, interest was aroused in the solitary of the Pacific, and there were some who at last believed in his genius. Plans were made to commemorate his death at the Salon d'Automne, and Ambroise Vollard organized a great exhibition of his last works.

Since then curiosity and fame have grown ceaselessly around the name of Gauguin. Unfortunately, however, much of this fame is due to his colourful, dramatic life, whereas it is in his work that his genius should really be seen. It was through this that he wished to triumph, and through this he deserves to survive. It is by admiring it and penetrating its deep significance that we can serve Gauguin's memory as he himself would have wished.

TAHITI: OR THE ENCHANTER (1902)
LIÈGE MUSEUM

LIST OF ILLUSTRATIONS